WORK WITH CHILDREN and Young People

CONTENTS

FOREWORD

by Floella Benjamin, presenter of 'Play School

'Caring for children is probably one of the most important jobs anyone can do. People who work with children - whether they are helping children to develop through play, caring for children whose mothers are at work, looking after children's health, or helping children in trouble - are making an important contribution to the well-being of the next generation.

In my work with charities I see many children from difficult or disturbed backgrounds. The rising divorce rate and increasing number of children brought up in single parent households creates enormous stresses in children's lives. Yet even when children suffer from the most severe and distressing difficulties or handicaps, there is still hope that, with dedicated care, they lead fulfilling lives. And for those who care for such children, the work can be richly rewarding.

I hope that this book will prove to be a useful guide, not only for young people interested in working with children, but for older people too. Anyone who has

Floella Benjamin

brought up a family of their own has a wealth of experience to draw on - an invaluable background for working with children in a professional role. But whatever your age, if you enjoy being with children, you already have the most important qualification for an immensely satisfying career.'

INTRODUCTION

From birth to maturity, children and adolescents come into contact with a wide range of professional workers - from the midwife who delivers babies to the youth worker who helps teenagers adjust to the realities of adult life. 'Working In - Work with Children' introduces some of these professionals, concentrating mainly on those whose work helps children to develop physically, emotionally, intellectually and socially.

A job or career involving children is by no means easy. It is often children who are in trouble, physically or emotionally, who need the greatest attention. Children can be demanding, frustrating and exhausting; but, of course, they can also be stimulating, exciting and rewarding.

PERSONAL QUALITIES

To work with children, you need to be mature - this is not necessarily a matter of years, but of outlook. You need to be patient and tolerant, but firm and consistent in setting boundaries of acceptable behaviour. Children have to know where they stand, and to be sure that rules will be applied firmly and fairly. This can be difficult, particularly with older children and adolescents. Think of how an unruly class can make life a misery for a teacher who lacks self-confidence. You might have to deal with similar situations; would you be confident enough to cope?

Good communication skills are essential in work with children. You have to be a patient, attentive listener. You also need to be able to communicate at different levels. With children, your language must be clear and simple; but you also need to communicate with other workers, and in many cases, this means using complicated terminology. Child care professionals have their own jargon - you need to be able to switch between this and the ordinary, everyday language which children, and their parents, will understand.

Shared interests always help to create and sustain relationships. Do you have hobbies you can share with children - like sports or arts and crafts?

If you are interested in working with children, it is sensible to examine your motives. Is your desire to work with children somehow mixed up with your wish to become a parent? Most of us want a family at some stage in our lives, but this doesn't mean that we all have the skills, commitment and personal qualities to work with other people's children on a full-time basis.

It is helpful, before you commit yourself to a job or training, to spend some time as a volunteer - many organisations, like the Scout and Guide Movements, local churches, playgroups and holiday playschemes welcome additional helpers. Experience of voluntary work will also demonstrate to potential employers that you are serious about your commitment.

MATURE ENTRANTS

Experience of life, including bringing up one's own family, is an advantage for many types of work with children. This is recognised in certain careers, by the lower academic requirements set for mature people applying for training. In social work and youth and community work, for example, the normal GCSE requirements are waived for applicants in their mid-twenties or above.

THE RANGE OF JOBS AND CAREERS

There are many areas of work which are concerned, to a greater or lesser extent, with children. A book of this length is necessarily selective. It features the experiences of a dozen people working with children and adolescents, mainly in a caring context. Within the areas covered - **working with the under-fives, health care, social work, librarianship, play and entertainment, youth and community work** - certain key roles have been highlighted. More information on these, and related careers, can be obtained from the organisations listed in the 'Getting In' sections. Remember, too, that the largest single career with children is the teaching profession - which is covered in more detail in a separate book in the 'Working In' series.

WORKING WITH THE UNDER-FIVES

In this country, services for the under-fives are limited, and vary from area to area. Generally, young children still spend most of their time at home, even though it can be of great benefit, particularly for three and four-year-olds, to participate in educational and play activities outside the home. Many parents too, would like to return to work, if high-quality care were available outside the home.

Slowly, however, the situation is improving. Tax restrictions on workplace nurseries have been removed; enlightened employers are beginning to set up their own nurseries, or to provide other forms of subsidised childcare; and an increasing number of private nurseries are opening. The potential demand for childcare from working parents is enormous, so there are likely to be increased job opportunities, over the next few years, for people trained to care for young children.

There are several main career and job options for those who are interested in working with the under-fives. They can choose to work in a care setting, like a day nursery or crèche, where they will be involved in both the practical aspects of looking after children and in helping them to develop, primarily through play activities. Care-givers also work in private households, as nannies and parents' helps, and in their own homes, as registered childminders.

Alternatively, work with the under-fives can take place in an educational setting - a nursery school or nursery class in an infant, first or primary school - where the emphasis will be on developing the children's interests and abilities. Most children attend nursery classes on a part-time basis, and because they are there for a short period, more time is spent developing their intellectual, emotional and social abilities, and there is less involvement in the practical aspects of childcare.

Another option, which is growing in importance, is to specialise in play activities. This does not necessarily mean working with children under five, and is therefore covered in a separate section of this book (page 19). But for all those who work with the under-fives, play is a fundamental concern.

In the following pages, we look at three distinct roles: nursery nursing, teaching the nursery age group, and childminding. All these have elements in common, but despite the similarities, the training, approach and emphasis are different in each case.

NURSERY NURSING

Nursery nurses work with young children in a variety of settings, including:

- **Day centres for the under-fives**. These

include local authority nurseries and family centres (where the staff are known as nursery officers); crèches, often subsidised by employers; nurseries run by voluntary bodies; and privately-owned day nurseries. Some nurseries give priority to children from vulnerable families; other, particularly in the private sector, cater mainly for the children of mothers who have returned to work.

- **Nursery schools** (and nursery classes in other schools). Nursery nurses work alongside teachers, assisting with the children's educational programme.

- **Private homes**, as nannies. Nannies often live with their employers, although some live-out posts are available. There are opportunities for nannies to work abroad.

There are also some opportunities for nursery nurses to work in hospitals, but they are not specifically trained in the care of sick children, and there are other qualifications more appropriate for those wishing to work with children in hospitals - see 'Health Care', page 8.

Nursery nurses who qualify by passing the National Nursery Examination Board exams are known as 'NNEBs'. They are, in fact, trained to work with children up to the age of seven, although the majority of their work is likely to be with pre-school age children.

THE NURSERY OFFICER

There are, as yet, very few men in nursery nursing, but the prospects for those who enter this type of work are good. It is now understood that even very young children benefit from having plenty of contact with both men and women, and many employers are keen to take on male staff.

Peter Jordan, who recently qualified as an NNEB, was one of only two students on his course - both men - to find work in a local authority run nursery. (Local authorities generally offer better pay and career structures than other employers of NNEBs).

Peter Smith

Peter did not go into nursery nursing directly after leaving school. He made a couple of false starts - first teacher training, then university - but did not complete either course. It was only after a year as a voluntary worker - working mainly with children in playgroups and nurseries - that Peter found what he really wanted to do, which was to work with the under-fives. Having made this decision, he enrolled on a two-year NNEB (National Nursery Examination Board) course.

'The NNEB course combines different aspects of child care - like social work, health and education - and that appealed to me because I was interested in the idea of working with the whole child. In nursery nursing you're dealing, on a practical level, with all the child's different needs. I was also attracted by the strong practical element of the course. In my case, it included placements at a community nursery, a social services Family Centre, reception classes in a school, a special school and a private family - these are representatives of the different areas in which you can work.'

After finishing the course, Peter worked for some months in an inner-city nursery, where he found himself dealing with 'the most distressing aspects of what's happening in children's lives.' He worked with children who had suffered from abuse of various kinds, and with children with special needs. The job was stressful, and sometimes Peter found himself worrying about whether he could cope, but he did feel that he was making a substantial difference to the quality of the children's lives.

Peter now works at Chapelfields Children's Day Nursery, one of many nurseries being set up by the Midland Bank, in partnership with other organisations. In this case, the bank's partner is the local council. Some of Chapelfield's 48 places are reserved for the children of the bank and council workers, and the rest are open to the public.

Chapelfields is a new, purpose-built nursery, set in peaceful surroundings in a small park. Like all nurseries for the under-fives, it has a generous staff-child ratio - one worker for every four children under $2^1/_2$, one for every five older children. When we visited, the nursery had recently opened and not all the nursery places had been filled, so Peter and his co-worker, who look after toddlers in the $1^1/_2$ - $2^1/_2$ age group, had just three small boys in their care. Eventually, they will look after a group of eight, each taking special responsibility, as "key workers", for four children.

Peter and the other nursery officers work on a shift system, starting at either 8 am or 9.30 am, and finishing at 4.30 pm or 6 pm. The day starts, for staff on the early shift, with preparation - sterilising the bathroom, wiping down the nappy-changing area, and setting up the room in which the children are to spend their day, with a variety of toys ready for free play. The children arrive at around 8.30, and Peter settles them down and talks to the parents. 'We try to encourage the parents to relax,' he explains, 'which helps the children to settle, but sometimes this isn't possible, because the mothers and fathers have to rush off to work.

'The children are usually involved in free play until they've settled down, and then at about 9.30 they have a break for a drink and biscuit. Then we have some sort of structured activity - making something with craft materials, for example. This would only take up a short space of time, because toddlers have a short concentration span. After that we might have a story, or go for a walk, or watch a television programme.

'By about half past eleven the children are tired, so we get them ready for lunch, clear everything away and change their nappies (we also do this throughout the day, of course, as necessary). Then they're ready for lunch, and after lunch they sleep for about an hour.

'The afternoon seems much shorter - we have more free play, perhaps a structured activity, and tea at about four o'clock. Then the children usually go home at about 5.30, and we clear up.'

Whilst each day has a basic routine, there is no rigid pattern. 'You have a structure to the day, but with our age group it's as flexible as possible, so you're responding all the time to the different needs of the children. Also, you're looking closely at each individual, and how they need to develop.'

Chapelfields is a happy, peaceful place, and the children, although they have their own difficulties and needs, present few serious problems. Peter points out that nursery nursing isn't always like this. 'Working with children is not just about working with happy children, and it's not just about play. It's also about working with parents and other adults, and it makes demands on you, both physically and mentally.'

Peter feels that nursery nurses often tend to underestimate their capabilities. 'They're very talented and very skilled, but they could be more ambitious, and develop a greater sense of their own worth. Some people seem to think that nursery nursing is just a soft option for young women - we've got to get away from that idea.'

GETTING IN

England and Wales: *the most widely recognised qualification is the* ***National Nursery Examination Board*** *Certificate in Nursery Nursing (usually known as the* ***NNEB****). There are no set entry qualifications for the course, although some colleges require two or more GCSEs (A-C). Students are accepted from the age of 16.*

Colleges of further education and some private colleges run two-year courses for the certificate. Some three-year part-time courses are also available.

Some colleges offer courses for the two-year ***BTEC National Certificate or Diploma*** *in Caring Services (Nursery Nursing). Entry is with four GCSEs (A-C) or equivalent.*

Relevant qualifications are also awarded by the National Association for Maternal and Child Welfare (NAMCW), following a two-year training course. However, this qualification is not so widely recognised by employers as is the NNEB, and may restrict possible choice of jobs.

(Note: correspondence courses are also available, but they do not normally lead to recognised qualifications).

Scotland: *students take* ***SCOTVEC National Certificate*** *modules, leading to registration with the Scottish Nursery Nurses' Board. The programme of education and training normally lasts two years. No specific entry requirements are laid down.*

Mature Entry: *applications from older people are welcome. A shorter training period may be possible for those with previous relevant experience.*

NVQs: *at the moment, rapid changes in qualifications and training are taking place. At the time of writing, National Vocational Qualifications (NVQs) or Scottish Vocational Qualifications (SVQs) in Nursery Nursing are not yet available, but they are being developed.*

Further Information

The National Nursery Examination Board, 8 Chequer Street, St Albans, Hertfordshire AL1 3XZ.

The Scottish Nursery Nurses' Board, 6 Kilnford Crescent, Dundonald, Kilmarnock, Ayrshire KA2 9DW.

National Association for Maternal and Child Welfare, 1 South Audley Street, London W1Y 6JS.

THE NURSERY TEACHER

Kathryn Bailey teaches two classes of four year olds, each with about 20 children; one class attends in the morning, from 9 to 12, the other for an afternoon session, from 1.15 to 3.15.

With small children, an informal approach is essential. Observing Kathryn's class, it looks as if they are spending a lot of their time just playing. But their play is carefully structured - mainly by the way Kathryn sets out the classroom before the children arrive, arranging equipment and toys for the activities she has planned. And in any case, with young children, it is almost impossible to draw a dividing line between play and learning. 'A child can take an activity as far as it wants,' says Kathryn. 'It could start off as a play activity and then perhaps, with the direction of an adult, develop into a learning experience.'

Developing the children's ability to use language is a vital part of the work, and comes into every activity, Kathryn feels. It is important to extend the children's ability to express themselves in spoken English - and this happens in the most natural way, through Kathryn's questions and involvement in their activities.

Kathryn Bailey

'Say, for example, they're in the hairdressing corner, and they're having a super time, and are really involved. I join in - having my hair put in rollers - but at the same time, I throw in a few ideas. I ask who's going to work in reception and whether someone's going to make an appointment. I enrich and develop the activity, in context, so it's not artificial.'

At nursery level, reading and writing, as such, are not taught. However, Kathryn does aim to make the children *aware* of the concepts of reading and writing - principally by reading stories, but also by doing some writing herself: for example, she writes down the children's speech and reads it back to them. Number work, too, is approached informally - through activities like sorting bricks, or computer games. 'It's so much fun,' Kathryn says, 'that they don't realise it's work.'

Kathryn feels that if children are really absorbed in something, then they can carry on with it for a long time. 'It constantly amazes me, how involved even a three-year old can become - particularly with something creative or imaginative.'

The children also carry out some simple topic work - a recent subject was health, and the difference between healthy and unhealthy food. To show the children what would happen to food, if it was kept for too long, Kathryn left a bottle of milk and a piece of bread out in the classroom for a week. 'I asked them to predict what they thought might happen, and then we saw what actually did happen. We were using our senses, to smell the milk and to see how it had changed in consistency.'

Experiments like this develop the children's natural curiosity about the world, and at the same time, teach them basic scientific principles, in an informal way.

The children's play activities extend into a wide range of areas, including crafts, gardening and even simple cooking. They also go on frequent outings. Kathryn takes them to the local shops, to buy ingredients for their cooking; they recently went to a farm, to look at new-born pigs; they go to the park, to feed the ducks; and a small group recently went to a museum.

Contact with parents is always helpful for teachers of any age group, but it is particularly important for nursery teachers. 'When children first start, parents are encouraged to stay as long as their children need them,' Kathryn explains. 'Then once the children are settled, the parents still bring them into the classroom every day, and we chat informally. If they're worried about anything, we can always find time to talk privately. I feel that to get to know a child, you've got to know the parents.'

Until now, Kathryn has taken sole responsibility for the class, although she has help from special welfare assistants, who work on a one-to-one basis with children with special needs. However, the school is about to be re-organised, and soon Kathryn will be working very much as a member of a team, together with another nursery teacher, two NNEBs (nursery nurses) and the special welfare assistants.

The length of service of the school's staff shows how satisfying working with this age group can be: Kathryn has been at the school for 14 years, ever since she qualified as a teacher, and the two NNEBs for almost the same length of time. Kathryn feels that'The longer I work here, the more fun, interest and stimulation I get from it.'

GETTING IN

Local education authorities, who are the main employers of nursery teachers, generally require them to have specialised, during their training, in teaching three-eight year-olds.

In England and Wales, *intending teachers need at least two A levels and three GCSEs (A-C), including English language and mathematics.*

There are two main training routes:

- a course leading to a Batchelor of Education (BEd) degree - usually over four years. This is the most common route for those wishing to specialise in the nursery age group.

- a degree course in a relevant subject, followed

by a one-year postgraduate certificate in education (PGCE). There are only a small number of PGCE courses offering specialisation in the three-eight age range.
Mature Entry: *opportunities are good; more than a third of new entrants to teaching each year are mature students, aged 25 or over. Contact the addresses below for details of special training schemes for mature entrants.*
Further Information is available from: TASC (Teaching as a Career), Room 4/25 Elizabeth House, York Road, London SE1 7PH.

Scotland and Northern Ireland: the system of training is rather different in Scotland and Northern Ireland. For further details, write to:

Scotland - The General Teaching Council for Scotland, 5 Royal Terrace, Edinburgh EH7 5EF.

Northern Ireland - Department of Education, Rathgael House, Balloo Road, Bangor, Co. Down BT19 2PR.

CHILDMINDING

Childminding involves looking after children, during the day, in one's own home. Most childminders are women with families, although it is possible for people without children to do this type of work. Childminding does, however, demand a mature outlook. It's also important to have a reasonable amount of space in one's own home and to provide a safe, positive and stimulating environment for children.

By law, all childminders must be registered with the local social services department. The number of young children they are allowed to care for is regulated: the limit is three children under five (including members of their own family). Additionally, they may, at present, care for any number of older children, after school or during the school holidays. (This will change in October 1991, when a limit to the number of children under eight will be introduced. The limit has not yet been announced, but the National Childminding Association recommends that childminders care for no more than three five to eight year-olds).

Childminders are self-employed, and agree on a fee - usually the local 'going rate' - with the child's parents.

THE CHILDMINDER

'If you leave your child during the day, you want to feel relaxed, and know that the child is being looked after in the right way,' says *Isoline Russell*, who has been a registered childminder for the past five years.

In the past - before registration of childminders was as carefully regulated as it is now - Isoline left her own small children with childminders, until one particularly bad experience with a careless minder left her determined to find some other way of looking after her family. Finding no acceptable alternative, she was forced to give up day-time work, and took a variety of evening and night jobs, to make sure that either she or her husband were always at home with the children. This experience, Isoline feels, now helps her to understand parents' feelings, and to be the kind of childminder she would have liked to employ, all those years ago.

Isoline's four older children have since grown up and left home, but she has one much younger child, six-year-old Nadine. Childminding attracted Isoline because it offered the opportunity to combine paid work with looking after her own child at home.

Isoline cares for three young children - Oscar, aged 2, Ciaron, aged 3 and Thomas, $2^1/_2$ - during the day. She also looks after three older children, and her daughter Nadine, before and after school hours, and takes them to and from school.

It's a long working day - starting at 7.30 in the morning and finishing around 6 pm, sometimes later. After the older children have been left by their parents, Isoline walks them down to school - which she finds good exercise, but 'horrible when it's raining'. The younger children arrive between 9 and 10, and Isoline chats to their parents, checking that all has been well at home.

'Then we try to get settled in. I usually have a blanket on the floor, with all the toys out - and we start from there - playing, or reading stories.'

Later in the morning Isoline usually takes the children out - to the park, or shopping, or to the local library, where the children's

Isoline Russell

librarian runs story-telling sessions. They then have lunch, and afterwards Isoline encourages the children to have a nap, although they don't always want to sleep. Later in the afternoon, they go down to school to collect the older children, and then, between 5 and 6 o'clock, their parents come and take them home.

Some days involve special outings - to the seaside, for example; and once a week, Isoline and the three toddlers go to a drop-in centre run by the local Childminders' Support Project. There, the children can meet playmates, and for Isoline there is a chance to socialise with other childminders - important, in a job which can be socially isolating.

The Childminders' Support Project, besides providing a meeting place, has helped in other ways. Not long after she started childminding, Isoline attended the project's part-time training course, which covered topics such as children's health and diet, first aid, play and toys, the business side of childminding, and assertiveness training (important for dealing with parents).

The project also runs a toy library, from which childminders can borrow a varied range of toys. Isoline can supplement her own collection of toys and equipment - which includes a climbing frame and inflatable pool in the garden, books and educational toys indoors - so that the children's play can be as varied as possible.

With a calm, relaxed outlook, and a deep love of children, Isoline inspires confidence in her caring skills. She feels that to do the work well, you need *time* - to live at a child's pace, not an adults. Despite the fact that she actually has a lot to do - with the school run, caring for the toddlers and older children, and, in the evenings, her own housework - Isoline gives the impression that she always has time for everyone.

The biggest challenge for childminders, Isoline feels, is the parents. Like anyone else, a childminder needs to know when she can expect to start and finish work, but not all parents stick to the arrangements. 'You find there are some parents who think they can leave the children whenever they want, pick them up whenever they want - even, sometimes, they say they haven't got the money to pay you!' (For this reason, the National Childminding Association recommend drawing up a proper contract with the parents).

Childminding is, at least in some respects, a business, and it offers one of the main advantages of working for oneself: independence. It is important to follow the local authority's health and safety policy and code of practice - for instance, no smoking, provision of stair gates, insurance - but within these guidelines, a childminder is his or her own boss.

As childminders are self-employed, they have to keep some simple records; Isoline makes a note of the hours each child is cared for, the payments made by parents, expenses, health information and important phone numbers.

Looked at from a business point of view, however, childminding is not well paid, especially when the costs like food, heating and wear and tear on one's home are taken into account. 'It's a lovely job at times,' Isoline says, 'but I think it could be better recognised and better paid.'

GETTING IN

No special qualifications are required for childminding, but registraton involves checks of your home, health and police record. To register, contact your local social services department. As well as giving you details of the registration procedure, they will also let you know about any training courses for childminders that are run locally.

Further Information is available from:

The National Childminding Association, 8 Mason's Hill, Bromley, Kent BR2 9EY and

The Scottish Childminding Association, 17 Middleton Drive, Milngavie, Glasgow G62 8HS.

HEALTH CARE

There are many health care professionals whose work includes caring for and treating children.

Doctors and dentists can specialise in working with children; alternatively, if they opt for general practice, they are still likely to spend a lot of their time treating youngsters. Likewise, physiotherapists and speech therapists work with children and young people - but they also treat adult patients.

Nurses can specialise in caring for sick children, or they can work with children and their families in the community, as midwives, school nurses or health visitors.

In this section we look at two health care professionals working in contrasting fields: a hospital-based sick children's nurse, and a health visitor, who is based at a local clinic, but spends a lot of her time visiting people in their own homes. Both of them stress the importance of dealing with the family, as well as the children - so even here, the work involves children and adults.

Ann Bullen, whose work as a health visitor is described below, is almost entirely concerned with under-fives and their families; but health visitors in other areas, may work with all age ranges.

THE HEALTH VISITOR

Ann Bullen is based at a health clinic in a small market town. She is responsible for a caseload of 300-350 families with young children, and a handful of families with older children; she also runs regular clinic sessions, both in town and in outlying villages. Her work concerns the promotion of healthy living.

Flexibility is the keynote of much of Ann's work - both in terms of how she decides to organise her time, and how she deals with her cases. 'You are your own boss,' Ann says. 'You have your workload, you have a framework of basic policy, suggesting how often you visit, and what you check on: but within that, there is a lot of scope for individual choice and self-management.'

Following local policy guidelines, Ann visits mothers and children in their own homes, at regular intervals. She takes over from the midwife about 11-14 days after a baby is born, making weekly visits until the child is six weeks old.

'From there, we invite the mother to come to clinic, whenever she chooses. It's all done very much as a contract between the health visitor and the mother - I stress the importance of individual needs, so that mothers don't feel they're being bullied. Some of them don't want to come to clinic, and others come week in, week out.'

As each child grows up, Ann carries out assessments of developmental milestones - such as the ability to sit unsupported, to crawl, stand, walk and talk. Equally important is the assessment of the child's social, intellectual and emotional development, and of the mother's health and welfare.

It would be misleading, however, to see the health visitor's job simply in terms of carrying out a series of checks. As Ann explains, 'There is also what I would call the true health visitor role - which I find far more rewarding and interesting - the relationship with the mother, and the family, and sometimes helping them through periods of crisis.

'At the moment, for example, I am visiting a woman who has been diagnosed as having multiple sclerosis. I know her because she has a three-year-old, but I'm not doing anything for the child, other than seeing him for his regular developmental checks. What I *am* doing is helping that mother to come to terms with her illness, and making sure she gets referred to all the appropriate agencies that can help her.'

Referring families to other sources of help is an important part of the health visitor's work. 'If either the health visitor or parents have any worries, then we know where to refer the problem. For example, it may be the GP, the dentist, the physiotherapist - or, with a social problem, social services.

'When there are lots of stresses in the home, you are someone the family can turn to. You can arrange for a package of care. For instance, if the child is playing up, you can refer to playgroups and agencies working with the under-fives. Or you can arrange for the child to be cared for by a childminder for a few hours a week, to give mother a break, or for a family aide from social services to go in and help.'

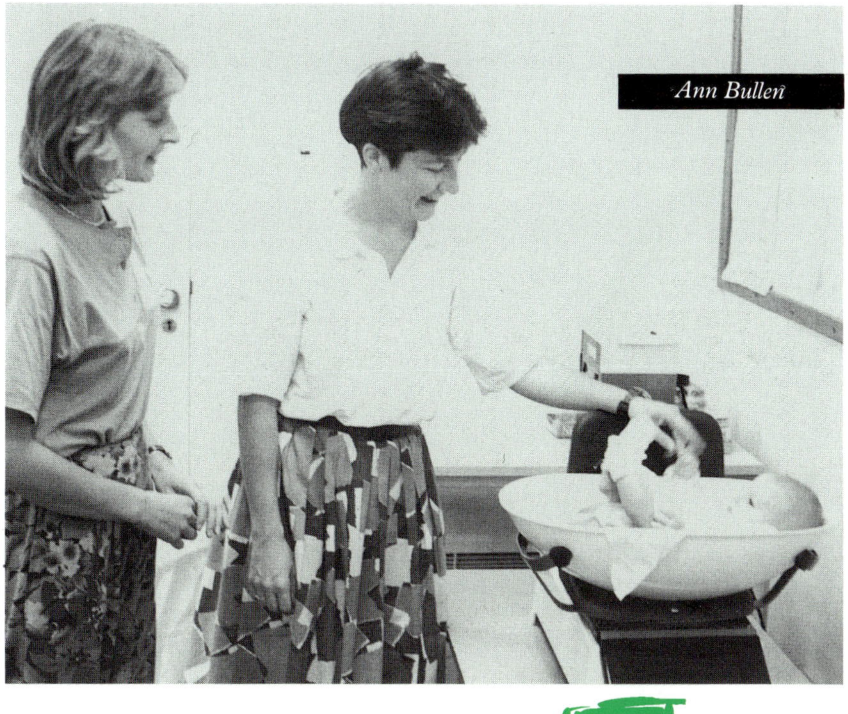

Ann Bullen

The essence of the job, Ann feels, is communication - both with other professionals and with families. It is also essential to build up trust. 'When you go in to see a family that you've never met before, with a new baby, you're trying to establish a relationship with them that may last ten years, if they have more children. You have to be very sensitive to their needs, and take the lead from them.'

When visiting people's homes, Ann only occassionally encounters hostility - when this happens, it is not usually from the mother, but from other members of the family. Often however, she comes across families whose standard of childcare is poor. In these cases, Ann has to work *with* the family, using her powers of persuasion to achieve whatever improvements are possible. 'There are grey areas,' Ann says. 'We all have our standards, but you realise that other people don't share them. You're talking about compromise. The mother may not be able to achieve all that you'd like her to, but if she can make just one of the changes you've suggested - that's progress.'

Ann's work is a combination of home visits, office-based administration, liaison with other agencies and clinic sessions. She also runs ante-natal classes, which is the only aspect of the job which involves evening work; otherwise, she works a normal Monday to Friday week.

Ann came into health visiting by a rather unusual route. She left school at 18, took a year off, which she spent working with physically handicapped people, and then went to university to study English Literature. It was only towards the end of her degree course, when she looked at her career options, that she decided to train as a nurse - influenced by her experience of caring for handicapped people, which she had found rewarding.

At that time, Ann knew very little about health visiting, and she saw basic training as a Registered General Nurse (RGN) as a pathway to a variety of jobs. Once she'd started training, she quickly decided that she wanted to work in the community, rather than in the more formal hospital setting.

Part of the RGN training involved working with a health visitor, and this proved to be decisive for Ann's choice of specialisation. 'Once I realised what a health visitor did, I thought "That's the job for me!" '

Qualifying as a health visitor, however, meant first gaining some experience in general nursing, then taking a further year's training.

Now, two years after qualifying, Ann is sure that she made the right decision. One of her few complaints about health visiting is that people often don't understand what she does. 'People seem to think that health visitors swan around smiling at healthy babies and chatting to mothers over cups of tea. There's so much more to it - it's all about communication, and that is what takes up so much energy, and time.'

GETTING IN

Health visiting is a post-registration qualification - this means that it is essential to gain a pre-registration general nursing qualification before you can train as a health visitor. It is also usual to have some experience as a qualified general nurse before you apply for the one-year health visitor course.

Further Information about careers in nursing is available from the following:

In England: English National Board for Nursing, Midwifery and Health Visiting, Careers Information Section, PO Box 356, Sheffield S8 0SJ.

In Wales: The Chief Nursing Officer, Welsh Office, Cathays Park, Cardiff CF1 3NQ.

In Scotland: The Nursing Adviser, Scottish Health Service Centre, Crewe Road South, Edinburgh EH4 2LF.

In Northern Ireland: The Recruitment Officer, National Board for Nursing, Midwifery and Health Visiting for Northern Ireland, RAC House, 79 Chichester Street, Belfast BT1 4JR.

THE SICK CHILDREN'S NURSE

Helen Cooper always knew that she wanted to work with children, but she wasn't sure whether to go into teaching, nursing or another career. Having left school at 16, Helen spent some time deciding what to do - she worked temporarily in an office job, then went to college to take A levels. Eventually, she decided on children's nursing, and at 19, started an integrated training course, leading to both the RSCN (Registered Sick Children's Nurse) and RGN (Registered General Nurse) qualifications.

Now, four years after qualifying, Helen is a staff nurse on a 22-bed children's ward, caring for children up to the age of about 14. A lot of her work also involves the children's parents, who are encouraged to stay in the hospital - and to sleep there - whilst their children are sick.

Parents are encouraged to become involved in the practical aspects of caring for their children - in terms of feeding, bathing, play and so on. The ward routine is very flexible; as far as possible, children follow the same timetable as they do at home, with the same bedtimes and bathtimes (although mealtimes, unfortunately, can't be varied).

The length of the children's stay in the ward varies considerably. Some are just in for a day, others are there for six to eight weeks, or longer. The average stay is about a week; Helen gets to know a child - and its parents - quite well over that period. During longer stays, a very close relationship can develop.

This closeness, however, has its disadvantages, because nursing sick children can, at times, mean dealing with tragic cases. A young girl was recently admitted to Helen's ward with suspected appendicitis, but later, an abdominal tumour was diagnosed. 'This affected the parents, and everybody else, really badly - it was very distressing. She had an operation, and she's making good progress now, but we're still concerned about whether she's going to get better.'

However, although children's nursing does involve coping with serious illnesses and

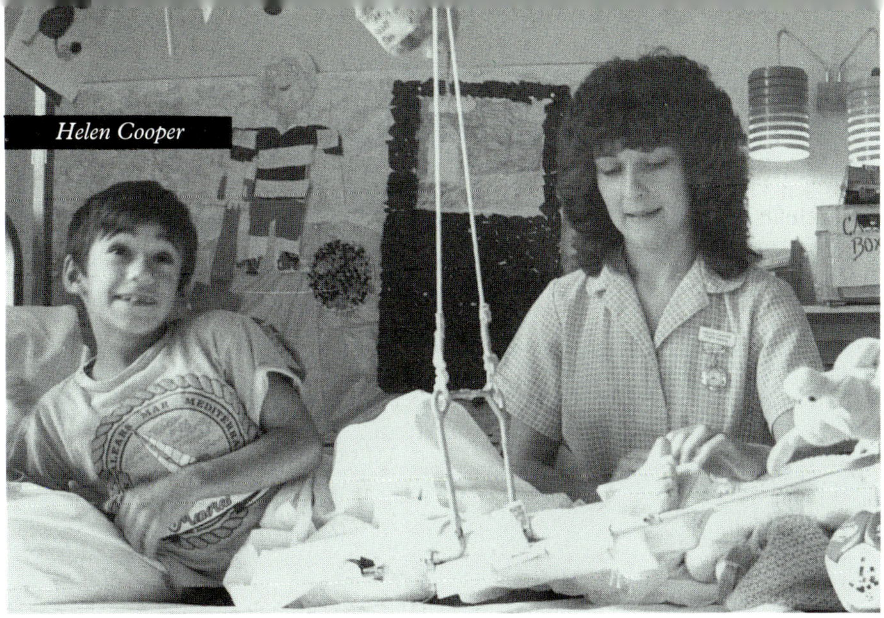
Helen Cooper

injuries, and - occasionally - with the death of a patient, children usually recover much more rapidly than adults.

'I prefer nursing children, because if they're feeling better, they're up and away,' Helen says. 'There's no in-between stage; they're either quite poorly, or full of life. Whereas adults, I think, tend to think about their illness for longer than children do, perhaps because they are more aware of its consequences.'

As a staff nurse, Helen is sometimes the most senior member of the nursing team, in which case, she is responsible for the whole ward. But if a sister is on duty, then Helen concentrates on nursing a small group of up to six children, dealing with every aspect of their care. She finds, in her present post, that she is responsible for making many of the day-to-day decisions about her patients - although, in Helen's experience, the amount of responsibility given to nurses does vary considerably from hospital to hospital.

Teamwork is essential in hospital nursing of any kind, and children's nursing is no exception. Although she takes primary responsibility for her own group of patients, Helen works with her colleagues, throughout the ward, as necessary. There is also close co-operation with other professionals - doctors, physiotherapists, teachers, social workers and the hospital liaison health visitor, who ensures that the community health care team are ready to help once a child leaves hospital.

Working as a team member means that communication skills are essential. 'You need to be able to communicate with children *and* adults,' Helen feels. 'You've also got to be sensitive to children's feelings - you shouldn't say that an injection won't hurt when you know very well that it will! And I think, too, that you've got to be cheerful, even when you're feeling rotten.'

Helen works a rotating day shift, either from 7.30 am to 3 pm, or from 2.45 pm to 9.30 pm. She never works nights, because in this particular hospital, there are permanent night staff. Every other weekend, however, Helen is on duty - with compensating days off during the week. 'It's something you get used to. Quite often it's nice to have a day off during the week, although it can be difficult working on Saturday and Sunday if all your friends are free. But children aren't only sick from Monday to Friday!'

Since Helen qualified, she has been continually finding out more about various specialisms, and picking up new skills and techniques. 'Things are changing all the time in nursing, with new ideas, new research. So you have to keep up-to-date - and you never stop learning.'

GETTING IN

Qualifying as a Sick Children's Nurse

Nursing education is going through a period of major change. A new system, called Project 2000, is being introduced - but it will take some years before it has completely replaced the existing method of training. For the time being, therefore, there will be two ways of qualifying as a nurse - Project 2000 and the existing system. *

Project 2000 *courses include an 18-month common foundation programme, followed by a choice of four 'branch programmes' - children's nurisng, nursing of adults, mental health nursing or nursing people with a mental handicap. Students who successfully complete the three-year course are qualified as registered nurses in their chosen branch, and are awarded a diploma equivalent to the first two years of a degree-level course.*

The present system *of qualifying as a sick children's nurse involves* ***either*** *a three-year course for the* ***Registered General Nurse (RGN)*** *qualification, followed by a further one-year course for the* ***Registered Sick Children's Nurse (RSCN)*** *award,* ***or*** *a combined* ***RGN/RSCN*** *course, lasting three years eight months. (The combined course is not available in Scotland).*

There is also a course leading to a degree and RSCN award, offered by Oxford Polytechnic.

Entry Requirements *for both types of basic (or 'first-level') nurse education are five GCSE/S-grades (A-C/1-3). A levels or H-grades are an advantage, but not essential. You must be* $17\frac{1}{2}$ *when you start training, although you can apply at* $16\frac{1}{2}$*, provided your exam results are known.*

Mature Entry: *there are no upper age limits for entry to nursing, and an increasing number of part-time courses, particularly suitable for people with family commitments, are available.*

* *Project 2000 will be the only way of qualifying in Scotland by the autumn of 1992, and in Northern Ireland, by March 1991.*

SOCIAL WORK

Caring for children at risk - and their families - means facing up to distressing situations and emotional pressures. It demands professional training, maturity, sensitivity, judgement and clear thinking.

These qualities need time to develop, and so social work, and related jobs in social care, are often best suited to people who have already gained some experience of life. Indeed, it is not possible to begin social work training until either 18 or 20 (depending on the course), and older people are often preferred.

Social workers are employed mainly by local authorities. Other employers include voluntary agencies ('voluntary' does not mean that the workers are volunteers - rather, that the agency is independent of government control), private organisations and certain official bodies.

The range of settings in which social workers practise is very wide; it includes offices based in local communities, hospitals, day centres, probation services, community work, education welfare services and a variety of residential settings. However, the two major branches of the profession are:

Field social workers, who work from offices serving the local community. They are responsible for a 'caseload' of clients whom they visit - this usually includes people of all ages, although often a large proportion of the work is with children and families.

Residential social workers, who provide care for children, and adults, who are living away from home in residential homes, hostels, schools and other establishments. In some cases, residential social workers live at the centre where they work, but very often they live out. They may, however, spend some nights 'sleeping in', and work shifts, including weekends.

There are also opportunities in the personal social services for staff at assistant, ancillary and unqualified levels. They are not trained social workers, but they are involved in working with children and their families in settings such as day centres, residential homes, child guidance clinics and education welfare services. Some may hold one of several awards, at a non-professional level, in social care.

THE FIELD SOCIAL WORKER

An outgoing personality and an air of easy-going optimism are qualities which help *Ursula Donnelly* to deal with the difficult and sometimes distressing situations she comes across in her day-to-day work.

Ursula is a 'generic' social worker. This means, in theory, that she is responsible for a wide range of people from different age ranges - not only children. In practice, however, the bulk of her cases do involve children, young people and their parents. Ursula's main aim is always to protect the children, wherever possible by keeping the family together, but if this fails, then she is responsible for organising fostering or residential care.

Although Ursula is office-based, she spends a lot of her time out visiting her clients. She sometimes makes seven or eight visits a day.

When visiting a family in difficulties, Ursula tries to get the family themselves to decide what their real problem is, and to work out possible solutions. 'I always say that I'm here to help, but I haven't got a magic cure,' Ursula explains. 'I just give them a helping hand over a difficult period.'

Amongst the 30-odd cases Ursula is currently dealing with, there are families where there has been physical assault - a parent beating a child - or where there has been sexual abuse, and a child has been removed from home for their own safety. There are also children and young people who play truant from school, or break the law; children in residential homes and foster care, who need

Ursula Donnelly

regular visits; and children who have returned from care to their parent's homes, whose progress is carefully monitored.

Ursula describes one particular case as 'high profile'. It involves a mother with limited capabilities, a father with a previous conviction for an offence against a child, and their new baby. To do everything possible to keep the family together - whilst making sure the child is safe - Ursula visits at least once a week. Just as important is the practical help and support which she organises, enlisting the help of other people concerned with the family.

'In a situation like this, you have a child protection case conference, where all the professionals - police, the health visitor, GP, probation service - everyone concerned with the family - is present. You discuss it fully with your Practice Manager, and you put up a safety net - weekly visits by the social worker, regular medicals on the child, a nursery place, lessons in basic parenting skills for the mother. In this case I feel that everyone involved has done their utmost to safeguard the child.'

Cases of this kind can be very stressful, and the pressures sometimes spill over into private life. Even though Ursula gets involved in outside interests - especially sport - to take her mind off work, she does find it difficult to 'switch off' in her free time.

'Every so often, a case does come to mind - you can't always shake it off. For example, just before Christmas I had to tell a mother that we were going to terminate her access to her child, and arrange adoption. It completely ruined Christmas for me.'

Although Ursula's work concerns parents, as well as children, she makes it a priority to listen to the child or young person's point of view. Often, she finds it helpful to take the child out somewhere - to MacDonald's, for example - for a private chat, away from parents or foster parents. If something is bothering a child, then it's much easier to talk about it outside the home.

Visits to clients take up over half of Ursula's time. Her working week also includes a regular day as 'duty' social worker: this means staying in the office, answering the telephone and dealing with anyone who comes in for help. Then there are meetings, court hearings to attend, and a ever-increasing amount of administration work. 'I probably spend the equivalent of a whole day a week on it,' Ursula complains.

Like many social workers, Ursula came into the job after doing other types of work - and, more importantly, gaining some experience of life. Social work, probation or the police service appealed to her when she was in her early teens, but she temporarily gave up these ideas after leaving school at 16 with a few CSEs. She then had a variety of jobs, including touring with a children's theatre, working for the local council, Thomas Cook's, and, in between, casual bar work. But she was still attracted to social work, and eventually, in her mid-twenties, applied for a job in a residential home for young people.

Encouraged by a supportive manager, Ursula then went on to qualify as a social worker via the Certificate in Social Service (CSS), an employment-based course for people working in social services.

'I decided to take the course, not so much for the piece of paper, but for my own personal development. I can't say I'm really academic, but I enjoyed doing the course, and its opened my mind. I think some people are put off because they think you need a BA or an MA to become a social worker, but if they've got an interest, then they should have the confidence to go for it.'

Once she'd qualified, Ursula moved from residential to field social work. In some ways she misses residential work: 'In a children's home you build up a relationship with the kids a lot more, whereas as a field worker you're in to sort out crises, then you're out again.

'Also, in field work, you may be taking action which results in the child going into care, so you can be the target of hate and resentment. I've had threatsn and verbal abuse; I haven't been hit, but it does happen.

'You wear two different hats. One is the caring, social work role - the supporter, the enabler; the other is that of the professional, working within the framework of the law. Sometimes, promoting the welfare of children means saying things that people don't want to hear, or removing a child from its home. You're torn between the two roles, but that's that job. You can't afford to be sentimental.'

THE RESIDENTIAL SOCIAL WORKER

Barnardo's has been caring for children in trouble since Victorian times, but in recent years the emphasis of the charity's work has changed. The orphanages of the past are gone, replaced by services geared to the needs of children, teenagers and their parents in today's world.

Amongst the charity's many concerns are the problems faced by children who, for emotional reasons, cannot cope with life in an ordinary classroom. For these children, Barnardo's runs a residential school, High Close in Wokingham.

A special educational programme, suited to the individual's needs, is drawn up for every pupil at High Close. Just as important - especially for the child's emotional well-being and self-confidence - is the school's residential campus, which provides a secure, caring, family-like environment. Although the children are boarders, they stay in close touch with their families, usually spending each weekend at home.

Vernon Nosal, a residential social worker at High Close, describes his work: 'I am a team leader for one of the residential units. I supervise four other staff, and we work together to provide a caring emotional environment for a group of eight children.'

Vernon Nosal

The work involves being constantly aware of each child's frame of mind and sensitive to their complex emotions. It is essential to talk through particular worries and problems - often connected with the family - which are affecting the child.

To help the children open up emotionally, each member of staff takes on 'key worker' responsibility for one or two children, and aims to build up with them a specially close, trusting relationship. At any time, a child can discuss particular problems and difficulties with the key worker; in addition, a specific period each week is set aside for the key worker and child to spend time together on a one-to-one basis.

The staff have to work hard to earn each child's trust. They have to demonstrate commitment by being prepared to work extra hours, or to make a special effort to organise outings or visits that are important to the child. Without gaining the child's confidence, Vernon feels, social workers cannot hope to influence their behaviour.

'It is also very important for us to define clear boundaries,' Vernon explains. 'Many of the children come from families which can't agree on the basic rules of behaviour - one parent will allow the child to do something, the other will forbid it. Here, the adults are consistent, and this gives the kids the reassurance that this is a settled and secure environment.'

A lot of the staff's work involves simply being available, in the children's home, and reacting to events as they occur. The day does have a structure, however. Mornings involve preparation for school - the children make their own breakfast, clear up and tidy their rooms. One member of staff then takes them to school, and lets the class teachers know about any problems that have arisen overnight.

Whilst the children are at school, Vernon and the other residential social workers catch up on paperwork, which includes keeping a daily record of each child's behaviour. They may also attend meetings with other staff and people from outside organisations. Another aspect of their daytime work is visiting the children's parents, with the aim of establishing a supportive, trusting relationship and discussing how the parents can help with the child's development.

Staff spend lunchtimes and evenings with the children; in the evenings they organise or assist with a range of activities. These include 'independence training' (helping teenagers with the skills needed for independent living) and sports such as swimming, football, cricket and snooker.

None of the staff live in, but they all have 'sleeping-in' duties, spending some nights (on a rota system) at the unit. They work shifts, but need to be prepared to be flexible. 'There are times when instead of finishing at five o'clock, we finish at eight,' Vernon comments. 'If the kids need something, you're there - there's no question about it.'

As team leader, Vernon's job involves additional responsibilities: he talks through, with individual members of staff, any problems they are facing in their work, and plans activities such as outings or sports events.

'If you've got some flair for sport, you'll normally get on with kids,' Vernon feels. It was his own keen interest in sport that originally brought him into social work. On leaving school, Vernon became an apprentice electrician, but with time on his hands at weekends, he also got involved in organising sporting events at Barnardo's project for delinquent teenage boys.

Vernon's voluntary work led to the offer of a full-time job with Barnardo's, and although by this time he had completed his electrician's apprenticeship, he decided that social work would be more fulfilling as a long-term career. 'Since then, I've never looked back,' he says. 'I've always enjoyed the work.'

After he had gained several years' experience, Vernon was seconded by Barnardo's, on full pay, to study on a two-year course leading to the CQSW - the Certificate of Qualification in Social Work. (It is rare, nowadays, for students on this course to be paid by their employers; most have to manage on a grant).

'It can be very rewarding work,' Vernon feels. 'It's not easy - I don't think anyone would pretend that it's easy to work with kids who have problems. You've got to have confidence, honesty and integrity - one of the worst things that can happen to these kids is to be lied to. At the same time, you've got to be sensitive - there are times when we have to break bad news gently.

'I think you've also got to have tolerance, warmth and affection. Some of these children are starved of affection: they've never had hugs or cuddles. If your reaction to a hug is to stiffen up, then you've rejected them.'

THE RESOURCE WORKER

Most social services departments welcome job applications from mature people with a broad experience of life, like *Joe Gordon*, who started work in a children's home at the age of 36.

'I spent a number of years in the army, most of them abroad,' Joe recounts. 'I then went into engineering, where I was setting machines, but I left after ten years because there was no chance of promotion, and I wanted to do something different, rather than be stuck in a factory.'

In the back of his mind, Joe had always been interested in some form of social work - preferably with children. He himself spent a brief period in a residential home when he was a child, and felt that this gave him some insight into the feelings experienced by children in care.

It was a chance meeting with an old friend from the factory, who was now working in a children's home, which gave Joe the impetus to apply for a similar job. He was accepted, and worked for a number of months as a night care worker in a home for teenage boys. He then progressed to a more responsible post after taking part-time training for mature entrants to social services work. (This particular scheme, run by Cambridgeshire Social Services Department, no longer exists. Other types of training are now available, including schemes leading to full professional social work qualifications.)

Joe spent a number of years as a child care officer, in several different children's homes. By a strange twist of fate, he actually worked for a time in the same children's home in which he had been placed, many years before, as a child - and found that it had changed enormously, mostly for the better.

Over the years he spent as a child care officer, Joe developed a special interest in preventive work with children and young people. He feels strongly that it is important to try to prevent problems occurring before the child reaches adolescence - by which time, it may be too late.

It was partly Joe's interest in preventive work, and his desire to broaden the scope of his career, that led him to take further training, via the *In-Service Course in Social Care*. This course, which is available nationally, aims to build on the experience of people who are already working in social services and related areas. It normally involves one day a week at college, over a year. The course can lead to promotion; from Joe's point of view, the opportunity to share experiences with people from different areas of social services was also valuable.

A chance to break into a new area of work came a few months ago, when Joe was appointed to a post at a resource centre for children, young people and their families. The centre, which is open during the daytime, has facilities for a variety of activities, like family therapy, individual counselling, direct work with children, and meetings.

Joe's post at the centre, as resource worker, is linked to the same children's home in which he stayed, many years ago. The home is now closing down, and Joe, together with another member of staff, are helping the children make the transition to foster homes, or to adoption. Joe's work also takes him into other areas, like other children's homes, or short-term fostering.

'The service is designed for the more disturbed children; the ones who've been in care a long time,' Joe explains. 'We do therapeutic work with the children over a

Joe Gordon

period of time, to diagnose the problem areas, work on these, and find foster parents to suit the child.'

One-to-one therapy sessions with the children, which generally last about an hour, may involve simply talking - or may be based around joint activities. 'Paintings, pottery, drawings and crayons are useful props because you can often get through to a child more easily by play - it's indirect.

'Our aim is firstly to establish a relationship, and to build up trust. Then, hopefully, we aim to get the children to talk about their feelings. We get to know the children, and what they want, and the sort of foster parents they would like. It's so important that we put children with people they want to be with. We ask them whether they want to stay near their school, whether they want to stay in the area where they grew up, how many other children they would like to be with, whether they want pets - all these questions need to be considered.'

Joe has regular meetings with key people in each child's life - teachers, foster parents, natural parents, residential social workers and others - both to gather information about the child, and to prepare the ground for eventual placement with a family. He also has paperwork to cope with - this includes writing detailed reports on each child.

After months of intensive work, Joe's efforts are beginning to pay off. When we visited the centre, we met two young boys - later, we learnt that one of them had just been placed in foster care, and the other is well on the way to finding a new home with adoptive parents.

Joe, at long last, has a real opportunity to put into practice his belief that 'All children have the right to live with a family, and we, as adults should respect that right.'

GETTING IN

There are three professional qualifications in social work:

CQSW (Certificate of Qualification in Social Work) *- a college-based course, most often lasting two years (courses lasting one, three or four years are also available for certain categories of student). You cannot begin this course until you are at least 20. If you are under 25, you need at least five GCSEs (A-C), including English language or Welsh, and preferably two A levels. In Scotland, two S grades (1-3) and three H grades, including English, are normally required.* ***If you are over 25, there are no formal entry requirements*** *- although you need to be capable of study at an advanced level. If you already have a degree, you take a one or two-year postgraduate course.*

CSS (Certificate in Social Service) *- this course is employment-based and lasts two-three years. You need to be employed by a social services department, voluntary social work agency or related organisation, be over 18, and provide evidence of academic and practical ability. If you are under 21, you also need five GCSEs or S grades (A-C/1-3).*

DipSW (Diploma in Social Work) *- this qualification will eventually replace the CQSW and CSS. The DipSW provides either an employment-based route to qualification, like the CSS, or college-based training, like the CQSW, or sometimes both. If you are over 21, the entry requirements are the same as for the CSS course. If you are under 21, you need two A levels, or four A/S levels, or three H grades, or NVQ/SVQ equivalents.*

For most courses, previous experience of paid or voluntary employment in social services is required, or at least strongly preferred.

Note: the last intakes to CQSW and CSS courses will be in 1994/5. Both awards will continue to be recognised as professional qualifications in social work.

There are also other courses for people working in social care, but these do *not* lead to qualified social worker status. They include:

The Preliminary Certificate in Social Care*: a two-year course based at colleges of further education. The course, originally designed for 16-18 year-olds, is intended as an introduction for those who are interested in working in the social services. There are no formal entry requirements. (In Scotland, this course has been replaced by the SCOTVEC Certificate in Social Care; in England, Wales and Northern Ireland, the last intake will be in 1991).*

BTEC National Certificate/Diploma in Social Care*: (two years full- or part-time). Entry is with four GCSEs (A-C) or equivalent.*

SCOTVEC National Certificate in Social Care*: the course usually lasts two years, but the length is flexible. There are no specific entry requirements.*

National Vocational Qualifications and Scottish Vocational Qualifications *in Residential, Domiciliary and Day Care (Levels II and III) are available.*

The In-Service Course in Social Care*: for staff involved in paid or voluntary work in social services. Typically, students attend college one day a week for one academic year.*

Further Information

Further information on training and careers in social services is available from the Central Council for Education and Training in Social Work (CCETSW) offices in:

London: Derbyshire House, St Chad's Street, London WC1H 8AD.

Edinburgh: 78-80 George Street, Edinburgh EH2 3BU.

Cardiff: West Wing, St David's House, Wood Street, Cardiff CF1 1ES.

Belfast: 6 Malone Road, Belfast BT9 5BN.

Children's librarians (also called youth services librarians) are responsible, in public libraries, for the children's library, and for encouraging teenagers and children to use the service. They run outside events such as story-telling sessions or book exhibitions, and visit various groups in the community to talk about children's books and promote the library service.

SCHOOL LIBRARIANS

The other main area of work with children is in school libraries. School librarians contribute to teaching programmes, including those which develop literacy and information handling skills. They also seek out and publicise information about books, other materials and sources of information. Having selected and obtained a wide range of materials for the school library, they organise and exploit these materials so that teachers and pupils use them to their maximum value for both educational and recreational purposes. A successful school library is one which pupils use not only for school work but also for leisure reading.

As in public library children's services, there is a direct relationship between school librarians and a wide range of people, including teaching colleagues, pupils, parents and school governors.

Alison Frost

THE CHILDREN'S LIBRARIAN

'Books are incredibly important for children, not only for their emotional and intellectual development, but also in terms of introducing them to different experiences and expanding their horizons,' says *Alison Frost*, children's librarian at a large city-centre public library.

'We're aiming to introduce children of all ages to a wide variety of literature. To encourage them to come in, and to want to stay, we make the library as attractive, exciting and lively as possible. We want children to be really drawn to the library, as a place of recreation - and also as a place where they can find information for school projects and for their own leisure interests.'

Alison's enthusiasm about the children's library is infectious; and it certainly is an attractive, inviting area. It is set apart from the adult section, up a flight of stairs, and has an informal, friendly atmosphere. As far as possible, the facilities have been planned around children's needs - on the carpeted floor there are cushions to sit on, toys, and a playpen for toddlers. When Alison reads a story to a group of small children, she sits down on the floor, comfortable at their level.

Like the adult library, the children's section has an enquiry point where children, parents and anyone concerned with children's books can ask for help and advice. Responding to enquiries is an important aspect of Alison's job - and it requires good communication skills and sensitivity to children, who may be shy about asking for help. Alison tries to find out exactly what children are looking for, shows them how the library works, and, if necessary, directs them to other reference sources in the library, such as encyclopedias.

Another important aspect of Alison's work is to organise regular activities in the children's library. These include story-telling sessions, visits from authors and illustrators, and games to encourage reading. During term-time, school classes come on visits; for them, there are special games and quizzes.

Another part of the job is purchasing and selecting stock - not only books for the children's library, which caters for the under-12s, but also for the teenage collection, housed in the main library. Alison aims to select a balanced collection of books for the various age groups and abilities. She has her own favourite authors, and one particular book she singles out for special praise is a new title about starting school. 'It's a wonderful introduction for the under-fives - it tells them what to expect when they go to school, and what school is going to be like *for a whole term*, not just for the first day. It brings out all the interesting and exciting things which children can expect.'

In promoting the library service, Alison works with other children's librarians across the county. As a team, they organise special events, like a summer scheme to encourage children to read widely during the school holidays, family reading groups and talks in schools.

Parents need to understand the tremendous value of wide reading if they are to encourage their children to make full use of libraries. So Alison - like other children's librarians - regularly gives talks to parents at playgroups, parentcraft classes and other organisations.

'We also take books out into the community, to book fairs, museum events and summer play schemes. We run story sessions; we also man exhibitions and use them as a means of promoting the library service. We take every opportunity to go out and take books to people, as well as trying to encourage them to come into the library.'

Anyone who is interested in a career as a children's librarian, Alison feels, obviously needs to be able to relate well to children, but also should be capable of communicating well with adults, especially parents and teachers.

'You need to be able to get across your enthusiasm and your knowledge of books. You also need organisational skills, not only for managing special events but also for the day-to-day activities of the children's library.'

Alison initially trained as a teacher, but went on to qualify as a children's librarian because she wanted to work with children in a less formal setting. She enjoys the work enormously, and says: 'I find it very rewarding to see children coming back again and again to the library, really eager to read. It's also rewarding when a child comes in, wanting some information, and goes away happy with what he or she has found and confident about using the library. What we're hoping is that those children we're introducing to the library at the earliest age are going to enjoy coming back, and using books, right through to adulthood.'

GETTING IN

Librarianship is now an all-graduate profession. There are two main ways of qualifying:

1. A degree in librarianship and information studies. Courses last three or four years, full-time; some longer part-time courses are available. Entry is with a minimum of two A levels/three H grades and three other subjects at GCSE/S grade (A-C/1-3), normally including English language (or equivalent qualifications). Detailed subject requirements can be checked with the university, polytechnic or college concerned.

2. A postgraduate course in librarianship and information studies. These courses usually last one year, full-time, although a number of longer part-time courses are available. Entry is with a degree - any subject may be acceptable, although some institutions may require specific subjects and/or class of degree. Most require applicants to have had about a year's previous work experience in a library or information environment. This need not necessarily be with children.

It is an advantage, although not always essential, to select a course offering an option in children's librarianship. This option is available at Birmingham Polytechnic, Ealing College of Higher Education, Leeds Polytechnic, Liverpool Polytechnic, Loughborough University, Manchester Polytechnic, Newcastle Polytechnic and the University College of Wales, Aberystwyth.

Mature Entry: *the part-time study route may be more suitable for mature entrants. If the nearest institution running librarianship and information courses does not appear to offer facilities for part-time study, it is worth making an enquiry, in case the possibility is being considered.*

Professional Qualifications: *Full professional qualifications are gained by becoming a Chartered Member of The Library Association (details are available from the Association). Many middle management and senior posts in the library and information sector are only open to Chartered Members of the Library Association. This particularly applies in work with children, which is mainly in public library and school library services, as employers in the public sector usually require applicants for such posts to be Chartered Librarians.*

Further Information, including a list of accredited degree and postgraduate courses, is available from the Education Department, The Library Association, 7 Ridgmount Street, London WC1E 7AE.

In modern society there are few places, outside the home, where children can play in safety. At one time they could play on street corners or in open countryside, but nowadays, traffic and other dangers mean that most younger children need constant supervision. Meanwhile their need to meet other youngsters and to discover the possibilities of the outside world, through play, remains as strong as ever.

Playworkers are employed to meet this need, and they run projects such as adventure playgrounds, after-school and holiday play schemes, and activity-based sessions like arts clubs or drama groups. There are a wide variety of jobs within playwork and many different job titles.

Increasingly popular, because they reach a large number of children, are playbus schemes, like the one described here.

Lynda Sexton and Gail Harbottle

THE PLAYWORKER

The Downham Market Community Playbus is a mobile play centre, serving a rural area. The bus is a lifeline for parents and children living in small villages where there are no nurseries, no playgroups and few places for children to play outside their own homes.

The playbus has two organiser/drivers, *Lynda Sexton* and *Gail Harbottle.* They drive the bus on its regular route, which takes in nine villages, and run two-hour play sessions at each stopping place.

'I like this job because we're on the move,' Gail says. 'Every session is different, we meet different people each time, and we're out in the community.'

The gaily painted double-decker bus has been specially converted for its new role. It is surprising to find how much has been fitted in. On the top deck there is a home corner, equipped as a child-size kitchen; an open, carpeted play space; and bench seats for adults, with storage cupboards underneath. Downstairs, behind the driver's area and door, are wipe-clean surfaces for activities like painting and modelling, as well as tanks containing those vital play ingredients - sand and water. Space has also been found for heaters, a sink and a lavatory.

Lynda and Gail find the layout of the bus lends itself to a natural division between mothers, babies and toddlers, on the top deck, and three to five year-olds downstairs. There is no hard-and-fast dividing line, and the children can freely go up and down the stairs, but generally the upper deck is for little ones to play as they wish, while their mothers sit and chat. Downstairs, activities are more structured, with opportunities for creative play, using Lego, building bricks, sand and water. And as well as these staple items, every week there is a special project, like craft work or finger painting.

For children who may have been very isolated, the playbus is a wonderful opportunity to learn to play with others, and to interact with adults, outside the family. 'Some of them have never played with another child,' Lynda explains. 'They perhaps live two or three miles from the nearest house, and they don't get to see other children. It helps mothers, too, because, they're often stuck at home all day, and don't see anyone except their child.'

Lynda and Gail explained that for some of these children, just talking to an adult who is not a member of their own family can be a completely new experience. At home, they may only get attention when they misbehave - not when they learn a new word, build a house with their bricks, paint a picture or develop any other talent.

The playbus is very new - at the time of our visit, it had only been running for six weeks. Gail and Lynda have been employed for rather longer: before they started running play sessions, they had a seven-week training period. Their training covered the operational side of running the bus: maintenance, safety and driving. No special driving licence is required, because no paying passengers are carried (the bus is stationary whilst children are on board), but obviously Lynda and Gail had to learn how to handle and manoeuvre the vehicle. During their training, they also observed an existing playbus scheme, chose books, toys and materials, and had discussions with child care professionals.

Both Lynda and Gail have children of their own, and feel that this is an important qualification for the job. They have also worked with children, Lynda as a childminder, Gail as a playgroup organiser. Lynda was a van driver at one time, so her blend of driving and child development experience makes her a natural for the post.

When Lynda and Gail applied to work on the playbus, they wanted to job-share. In the first few weeks, this wasn't possible; so far they have both been working almost full-time, with temporary help from a third worker, Philippa, who is on an Employment Training scheme. Soon, however, another permanent post will be created, and Lynda and Gail will share one full-time job.

The three workers will, between them, drive the bus on its regular weekly schedule, visiting nine villages, and share the Friday afternoon 'maintenance' session, where they clean the bus, check that it is in good mechanical condition, and plan the following week's work. There are also records to fill in, committee meetings to attend, cash handling (a charge of £1 per family is made for each session, with exemptions for those on low incomes) and liaison with other organisations. A further aspect of the work is fundraising - as the playbus project relies heavily on voluntary contributions, a continuous effort will be needed to raise the necessary finance.

For a project which has so recently got off the ground, the playbus is already well attended, with almost full capacity at each session. 'We hear that the children are always talking about the bus at home,' says Gail. 'They can't wait for it to come round again.'

GETTING IN

Experience of working with children, or of bringing up one's own family, is a useful background for playwork.

Training in playwork has, to date, mainly been arranged at local level, by employers. However, a national training scheme is being developed by the National Children's Play and Recreation Unit. Other courses include:

Diploma in Higher Education (Playwork): *a two-year full-time course at Leeds Polytechnic. The first year of the course is also offered at Thurrock Technical College; students transfer to Leeds in year two. The majority of entrants are mature applicants with experience in playwork, but younger people may be accepted. Academic entry requirements for younger applicants are five*

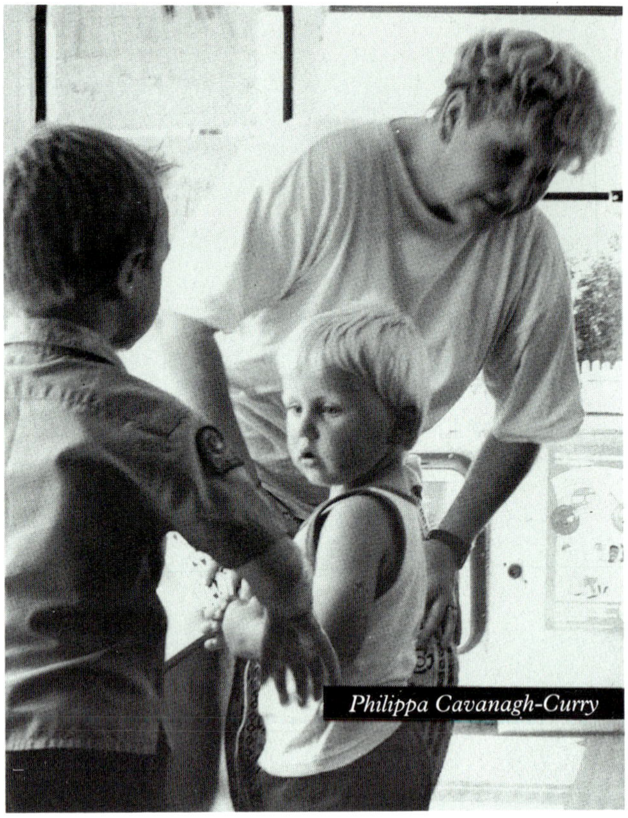

Philippa Cavanagh-Curry

GCSEs (A-C), and two A levels, or equivalent; these requirements do not apply to mature candidates.

Certificate in Playwork: *a one-year part-time course for experienced playworkers, offered at Birmingham Polytechnic and Charles Keene College of FE, Leicester.*

Pre-School Playgroups Association courses: *a variety of part-time courses, geared to local needs, are available for those interested in playwork with the under-fives. Many of those who work with playgroups are volunteers, but some paid posts - mainly part-time - are available.*

National Vocational Qualifications and Scottish Vocational Qualifications in Playwork are under development, at the time of writing.

Further Information is available from:

The National Children's Play and Recreation Unit, 359-361 Euston Road, London NW1 3AL.

The Pre-School Playgroups Association, 61-63 King's Cross Road, London WC1X 9LL.

THE CHILDREN'S ENTERTAINER

Len Sharp is affectionately known to thousands of children by his stage name, 'Uncle Len'. With his magic tricks, balloons and party games, Uncle Len is well-known in his local area as an entertainer at children's parties, playgroups and schools.

Len became a children's entertainer in a curious way. An experienced engineer, he started working with a firm called Hughes House of Magic, designing and making equipment used by magicians, like the boxes used to create the illusion of sawing a person in half.

Intrigued by the tools of the trade, Len started experimenting and playing around with magical tricks at home. Gradually he began to work up an act, and tried it out on friends and neighbours. Then, through his employers, he got his first professional engagement. Delighted, he packed up his tricks and arrived at the venue - only to be confronted by 600 children, waiting to be entertained.

'I just wasn't prepared for that number,' Len remembers. 'It was chaos! When you're entertaining, you have to be in control of everything that's going on, because background noise from mums, dads or caterers can ruin your act. But at this place, they were moving tables and giving the children ice-cream whilst I was trying to entertain. It was an absolute disaster!'

Undeterred by this experience, Len carried on entertaining, learning from his mistakes. Largely through word of mouth, he gradually built up a reputation for entertaining at children's parties. For some years, he was a semi-professional, combining work for Hughes House of Magic with his engagements. Eventually, he had enough contacts, and enough work, to go full-time.

At children's parties - his bread-and-butter - Len's act takes about an hour. He varies his routine a lot, but always includes some basic tricks including rabbits, which appear and disappear in unlikely places, and balloons, which he moulds into animal, flower and bird shapes. Audience participation is important, and Len's favourite way of getting the children involved is by making deliberate mistakes. The children's cries of 'Not there, not there!' or 'Silly Uncle Len!' are a sure sign that they're enjoying themselves.

Pace and timing are all-important in live entertainment, particularly when it involves magic tricks. 'You keep following on, all the time,' Len explains. 'You're always one step ahead of the audience. You have to keep them on their toes.'

'In this job you've got to love relating to children, and be outgoing, and have the gift of the gab,' Len says. 'You've also got to know yourself, and your own personality. I've developed my own act from start to finish - I think you have to be very careful not to copy anyone else.'

Len varies his act according to the age of his audience, and with very small children he keeps it slow and simple. 'With little ones it's very visual, very easy to follow. They love it, and they all feel safe. On the other hand, if you've got a teenage audience, then the pace is much quicker; they want to try and catch you out, so you have to keep moving.'

The bookings are a mixed bag - Christmas and birthday parties, playgroups and the occasional session in council parks, or holiday camps. Len also gives up some of his time, on a voluntary basis, to visit school assemblies and churches. On these occasions he uses his magic tricks to illustrate religious themes. 'They help people to remember the message.'

At busy times, like the Christmas period, Len's schedule is packed. He has done as many as ten engagements in one day, a feat which requires careful planning and precise timing. But like most self-employed people, Len goes through slack periods as well. From a financial point of view, this means he has to keep firm control of his earnings, resisting the temptation to spend when the going's good, so that he has sufficient to tide his family over in quieter times.

Advertisements in local newspapers bring in some of Len's bookings, but he finds his shows are his best advertisement. Children see Len at friend's parties, then persuade their parents to book him when their own birthdays come round. To make sure the parents know how to contact him, Len distributes 'magic money', stamped with his address and phone number, at the end of each show - a neat publicity move.

Some years ago Len used to tour, and he worked with one of the big names in magic, familiar to TV viewers. He is reluctant, however, to use this experience as a sales gimmick.

Len Sharp

'You can't rest on your laurels. Names don't mean anything - what matters, in this business, is whether the children are responding, whether your audience is with you, whether they like you. If they don't, you won't see them any more. As the saying goes, you're only as good as your last show.'

GETTING IN

There are several thousand children's entertainers in Britain - some working full-time, like Len Sharp, others who are 'semi-pros', combining a day-time job with weekend and evening engagements. Every entertainer's act is different, but most include some magic tricks in their repertoire.

If you are interested in this type of work, you can learn more about magic by joining your local magic club - most sizeable towns and cities have one. The address of the nearest club may be obtained by writing to:

The British Magical Society (Secretary: Dr Bob King), 20 Ragley Crescent, Bromsgrove, Hereford and Worcester B60 2BD or

The Secretary, The Magic Circle, c/o The Victory Services Club, 63-79 Seymour Street, London W2 2HF.

There are no specific training courses for intending children's entertainers/magicians, but some individual members of magic societies do offer training sessions on a private, fee-paying basis.

YOUTH AND COMMUNITY WORK

The majority of youth and community workers, who are employed by local authority education departments, work in youth clubs or youth and community centres. However, the scope of youth and community work has widened in recent years, and now includes projects working with young people in a variety of other settings, formal and informal; it also includes community work with people of all ages.

Youth work is also carried out by voluntary agencies such as the National Association of Boys' Clubs, the YMCA and the Scout and Guide Associations. These organisations - and local authority youth and community services - rely heavily on help from unpaid volunteers, but they also employ full- and part-time paid staff.

Part-time posts in youth and community work are more numerous than full-time jobs. Full-timers may be responsible for the management of a centre, staff recruitment and training, and the planning and supervision of the service. These aspects can take up as much, if not more of their time, as face-to-face youth work.

THE YOUTH AND COMMUNITY WORKER

Peter Smith is responsible for youth work and other community projects in a town of about 40,000 people. His main concern is a large community centre, which is used not only as a youth club, but also as a venue for a variety of other groups, from pre-school playgroups to pensioners' clubs.

As the only full-time worker at the centre, Peter finds a lot of his time is taken up with the management of staff and buildings, administration and general promotion of the youth and community service. However, within that framework, youth work - with an emphasis on 14-18 year-olds - is his first priority.

'During the main season - September to June - the youth club is open four nights a week,' Peter explains. 'There are usually about 40 to 50 young people here on any one night. They can use the whole of the building - the sports hall, the activity room with its pool and snooker tables, the coffee bar area, and the main hall, where we have activities like carpet bowls, darts, theatre, music and discos. They also use the small meeting rooms for activities like group discussions.'

To help with these evening sessions, and with the general running of the centre, Peter has a team of part-time paid staff and voluntary helpers, each with their own area of interest. 'What I've tried to do,' Peter says, 'is to build a team of staff who complement one another. It would be no good at all to have staff who were all keen on sports, or all male, or all interested in arts and crafts. We each take a different approach.'

Four years ago, when Peter took over the running of the centre, he found that the sports hall was very much the focal point of activity. Peter is himself a former PE teacher, so this suited him personally, but at the same time he felt the centre should be attracting a wider cross-section of young people. To achieve this, he has introduced art facilities and theatre groups, and set up a coffee bar.

Peter has also widened the scope of the youth centre's work by employing a part-time

Peter Smith

outreach worker, who goes out into the town and makes contact with young people wherever they congregate - in cafes, arcades, or the street.

The outreach worker has lately been concentrating on meeting teenage girls and listening to them talking about their problems - particularly difficulties they face in coming to terms with their sexuality. The girls were then invited to small group sessions at the centre. Outwardly, these sessions are based on all kinds of topics which may interest girls, because no one would come to events billed specifically as discussions on sex, AIDS, or contraception. These topics can be raised - with tact and sensitivity - in the course of another activity.

This kind of youth work, which goes beyond arranging sports and activities and attempts to address young people's problems, is often described as 'social education'.

'There are numerous definitions of social education, but I feel that it's about growth, about getting on with and tolerating people,' Peter explains. 'I also think we are trying to say to young people that some behaviour is acceptable, and some isn't. You can't moralise - all you can do is try to reason with the young person. You can ask them whether they understand the damage they are doing to themselves, or to others. There are grey areas, where we can't say "This is right and this is wrong" - although of course we can't condone law-breaking.

'I think youth workers are advisers, supporters, helpers and initiators of growth - but we're not moralisers, and we don't see things in black and white.'

Peter came into youth work after qualifying as a PE teacher and working for a year in a large comprehensive school. He enjoyed teaching, but found it frustrating, trying to organise sports activities for very large classes, in short lesson periods. As he had already gained some experience of youth clubs, both at college and whilst teaching, Peter decided that full-time youth work, using his sports skills, would be a more satisfying career.

At that time, teacher training counted as an entry qualification for full-time youth and community work posts (this is no longer the case). Peter felt, however, that an additional qualification in youth and community work would be valuable, and so he took a part-time diploma course, whilst in his first youth work post.

The first job involved responsibility for a mainly rural 'patch'. Peter ran a small youth centre, but much of his work was concerned with thirty-odd independent youth clubs, run largely by volunteers. A lot of his time was spent on advisory work, visiting local clubs and suggesting new activities, or arranging training for volunteers.

Peter's present job is quite different. He is principally concerned with the running of a single centre, where most of the surrounding town's youth activities take place - although he does still have a 'patch', and sometimes advises the organisers of independent clubs. In the main, however, his role is managerial, and over 80 per cent of his working week is spent on organisation and administration - with face-to-face youth work fitted in to the remaining time. He finds he always works more than his contracted $37^1/_2$ hour week, and like all full-timers in this field, he has a heavy commitment to weekend and evening work.

In four years, Peter feels he has been successful in attracting a wider cross-section of young people to the centre, but believes there is more to be done. 'You can't hide from the fact that the numbers of youngsters who actually use the youth and community centre are few, compared to the total population of young people. There are a lot of youngsters out there who aren't using it - some for very good reasons, because they have other interests, or belong to other groups. There are also other young people who could be encouraged to use the centre, if what they wanted was provided. But you can't respond to every need - you have to do what is manageable, within your budget.'

GETTING IN

It is now usual for people interested in a career in youth and community work to gain some experience in voluntary and/or part-time paid youth work, before applying for a training course.
In England, Northern Ireland and Wales, *most courses are for mature students (at least 21 years old, preferably 23 plus). Minimum academic entry qualifications are usually five GCSEs (A-C), although this requirement may be waived for*

those over the age of 23.

The following training courses are available:

1. Two-year full-time initial training courses in youth and community work.

2. One-year full-time postgraduate courses.

3. Part-time initial training courses, lasting three years.

4. Part-time postgraduate courses, lasting two years.

5. Degree courses in Community Studies (at Bradford and Ilkley Community College), Youth Studies (at St Martin's, Lancaster) and Youth and Community Work (at the University of Ulster).

6. A distance learning course, lasting three years, run by the YMCA National College.

There are also a very limited number of apprenticeship schemes, offering a combination of on- and off-the-job training, over a period of two years.

Teachers who qualified before the end of 1988 may be appointed without having specific youth and community work qualifications.

***In Scotland** it is possible to enter training straight from school, although maturity and experience of youth work are an advantage. Entry requirements for those aged 18-22 are four H grades; **or** three H grades and two S grades (1-3); or two H grades and four S grades (1-3). Older entrants with three H grades **or** two H grades and two S grades are accepted. Graduates and holders of certain professional qualifications may take a one-year course.*

*Courses of initial training for the **Diploma in Youth and Community Work**, lasting three years, are available at four colleges of education in Scotland. Entrants over 23, with appropriate experience, take a two-year course.*

Further Information is available from:

National Youth Agency, 17-23 Albion Street, Leicester LE1 6GD.

The Scottish Community Education Council, West Coates House, 90 Haymarket Terrace, Edinburgh EH12 5LQ.

ACKNOWLEDGEMENTS

Written and researched by Helen Steadman.

Photography by P Lynam Clough (photograph of Floella Benjamin by Keith Taylor).

With thanks and appreciation to the following organisations:

Chapelfield Children's Day Nursery
The Midland Bank
The Equal Opportunities Commission
National Nursery Examination Board
King's Lynn Nursery School
Southwark Childminding Support Project
National Childminding Association
West Norfolk and Wisbech Health Authority, Community Unit
Jenny Lynd Children's Unit, Norfolk and Norwich Hospital
The English National Board for Nursing, Midwifery and Health
Cambridgeshire County Council Social Services Department, Peterborough Division
Barnardo's High Close School
Central Council for Education and Training in Social Work
Norwich Central Library
The Library Association
National Children's Play and Recreation Unit
Downham Market Area Community Playbus
The British Magical Society
King's Lynn Youth & Community Centre
Central Council for Education and Training in Youth and Community Work